What Would Ken Do?

™

What Would Ken Do?

WHAT I'VE LEARNED FROM LIFE AND BARBIE

BY KARA NESVIG

RUNNING PRESS
PHILADELPHIA

Running Press
Hachette Book Group
1290 Avenue of the Americas, New York, NY 10104
www.runningpress.com
@Running_Press

First Edition: August 2025

Published by Running Press, an imprint of Hachette Book Group, Inc.
The Running Press name and logo are trademarks of Hachette Book Group, Inc.

Running Press books may be purchased in bulk for business, educational, or promotional use. For more information, please contact your local bookseller or the Hachette Book Group Special Markets Department at Special.Markets@hbgusa.com.

The publisher is not responsible for websites (or their content) that are not owned by the publisher.

Text by Kara Nesvig

Print book cover and interior design by Alex Camlin

Library of Congress Cataloging-in-Publication Data has been applied for.

ISBNs: 978-0-7624-8873-5 (hardcover); 978-0-7624-8874-2 (ebook)

Printed in China

1010

10 9 8 7 6 5 4 3 2 1

CONTENTS

. . . but do you *really* know Ken? Chances are you have some assumptions about my good friend, and I'm here to tell you, he has a lot of wisdom to impart.

You see, I've known Ken for a long time—more than six decades, to be exact. And in that time, I've come to discover that Ken has lots and lots of layers! He's smart, funny, talented (have you seen him Beach?), the world's best dancer, and a thoughtful friend. Sure, he's had his fair share of questionable fashion moments, but haven't we all? I know I have! But hey, they were cool at the time.

Under the great hair and flashy smile, there's a really sweet guy. There's a reason he's been part of my crew since 1961 and why I still enjoy hanging out with him, even after all these years. Though our story has evolved, Ken and I are forever linked—and I couldn't ask for a better partner and pal. You're going to love hearing all about what makes Ken, Ken, trust me. He'll fill you in on his friends, his dating philosophy, his favorite outfits, and how to be as cool and thoughtful as he is. Ken is a genuine guy—his heart is true.

Love, *Barbie*™

My Story
KEN 101

You're probably here because you want to learn all the Ken secrets. A good friend. Lover of Beach. A doctor. A lifeguard. A pilot. A teacher. A barista. A rock star. Someone who is kind, stylish, and suave. And that's just the beginning of my resumé!

I made my debut as original Ken in 1961, just a few years after Barbie herself. Barbie creator Ruth Handler named me after her son—a cool fact since she named Barbie after her daughter. (We were destined to get along!)

Let's get one thing clear—there is no Ken without Barbie, and I'm her number one fan. And as her number one fan, I'd love to let you in on all the things I've learned along the way about Barbie and myself.

My full name is Kenneth Sean Carson, but nobody calls me that. I'm simply Ken, and that's exactly how I like it.

BTW, I'm a Pisces, which means I'm kind, romantic, generous, and creative.

Yep, sounds a lot like me.

Over the years, I've worn a lot of hats... and bow ties... and cummerbunds... and roller skates... and short shorts. You name it, I've probably done it; there's a lot you can accomplish in 60+ years!

I've been to the fanciest events, rode shotgun in the pink convertible, hung out at the DreamHouse, chilled with Barbie and friends in Malibu, and learned a lot of great life lessons in the process. And I'm here to share them with you.

But who *is* Ken? Ken is everyone. He's me! He's you! We've all got a little Kenergy in us, and in this book, you're gonna learn everything you need to know about being the very best Ken you can be.

DREAM DATE KEN: We had a great time. Dream Date Barbie was everything . . .

TOTALLY HAIR KEN: Packaged with a bottle of hair gel, my luscious locks were always ready to impress.

EARRING MAGIC KEN:
An icon. A legend. A collector's item. If you know, you know.

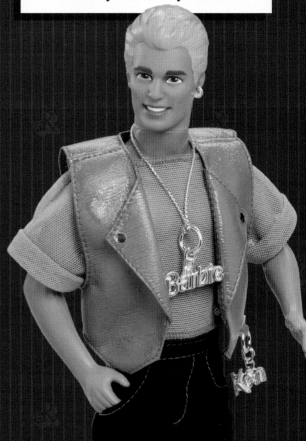

SHAVING FUN KEN:
Practice your barbering skills on my five-o'clock shadow!

10

ASTRONAUT KEN:
Boldly going where
Barbie has gone before.

**GOOD-LOOKIN'
TALKING KEN:**
His most important phrase?
"Let's go visit Barbie."

SUPERSTAR KEN:
Groovy doesn't even
begin to define it.

CRYSTAL KEN:
The handsomest Ken ever. Don't
believe me? Check the box!

What Kind of Ken Are You?

CULTIVATING YOUR INTERESTS AND TAKING CARE OF YOU

Sure, I've been labeled many things over the years. An accessory, a plus-one, arm candy. But I'm so much more complex than that. It's boring to be a one-dimensional person, and over the years, I've grown in many ways learning alongside Barbie, and I've developed real dreams and passions through all my different careers, hobbies, and adventures.

Forget what you've heard about me or how you pictured me with or without Barbie; Ken has his own thoughts, feelings, and interests. I am *so* not a sidekick. (Well, unless Barbie needs one—I'll happily be there. Sidekicks are very cool too.)

To figure out what kind of Ken you want to be, you need to narrow it down. What drives you? What makes you laugh? What inspires you?

You totally Ken do it!

Before you can find your own Barbie, either romantically or platonically, you gotta have interests and hobbies of your own. Maybe you play guitar — awesome. I used to play in a little band called the Rockers, maybe you've heard of them? Totally legendary if you ask me.

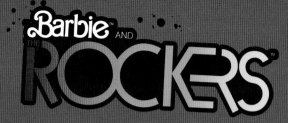

Perhaps you're a movie critic-in-training, filming your latest reviews. Or you love to ski and enjoy giving lessons!

Maybe you love to cook or join your friends every week for a mountain bike ride. Are you always doodling and painting in your spare time? Maybe you're an Artist Ken. Have a lot of pets? You should meet Animal Lovin' Ken, a real icon from 1988. Adventurous and outdoorsy? Camping Ken! An introverted bookworm? Maybe you're more of an Allan. And who wouldn't want to be Allan? Love that dude!

Don't be ashamed of your interests. They're what make you, well, you. People can sense when you're not being genuine; you're more likely to make new friends or attract positive vibes when you're fully yourself, so embrace what you like and who you are.

I Ken-NOT wait for you to try new things!

TIPS YOU SHOULD TRY OUT

Whether you're a Western Ken, a Fashion Model Ken, or a Business Ken, these are the skills you should definitely have in your back pocket.

1 Open yourself up to dancing with a partner. It's one thing to bust a move solo, but when you're dancing with someone, it'd be like, so cool to keep up without stepping on their toes. It's never a bad idea to take dance lessons to get the basics down. Ask Disco Barbie for a lesson or two.

2 Have a grasp on current affairs. You don't need to know everything about every single situation in the world, but keeping up with what's going on in the news is important and a great conversation starter. Ask News Anchor Barbie for help.

3 Can you tie a tie? A Ken like us may be more apt to don a bow tie than a traditional necktie, but you should still learn this skill just in case. The super glam Enchanted Evening Barbie has got your back here.

4 Learn how to eat nutritious foods. You don't have to become a professional chef, but self-care through food will boost your mental well-being and make it easier to be your charming, funny self. Learn how to whip up a few basic but delicious meals. Chef Barbie can help you hone your skills.

5 You can walk the walk, but can you talk the talk? We touched on this earlier but being a good conversationalist—whether it's with the person next to you in line, a new acquaintance, a coworker, or your best friend—is a life skill that pays off and opens doors. Ask Barbie for help. Any Barbie.

6 Learn how to keep the DreamHouse the dreamiest. From big projects to small, I've learned to tackle them all. Disco light show in the shower? Check. Build a puppy-sized pool and slide? Check. Save the backyard burgers from being charred? Double check! Those grill thermometers can be tricky! Whether it's unclogging a drain or installing a rooftop karaoke machine, you Ken do it! And Builder Barbie can help.

7 Care for your items and space. This means keeping your house clean and neat, laundering your denim vests and lamé trousers correctly, and upgrading your car, appliances, and cookware when necessary. Again, self-care rules! When you surround yourself with a peaceful environment, you'll feel more peaceful on the inside. Ask Interior Designer Barbie for tips.

8 Build a campfire and make s'mores. The Dream Camper is always ready to hit the road for the next adventure! And when it's time to wrap another epic day under the stars, nothing beats a cozy campfire, melty s'mores, and some cool acoustic sing-alongs. Ask Camping Barbie for help.

9. Enjoy hanging out with kids. Even if you have no kiddos of your own, you probably have a few little ones in your life. Midge and Allan have kids, Barbie has three sisters, and I have a lil' bro of my own, Tommy. Kids are *so* not a nuisance. They're creative, funny, and worth every minute of your time. Hang out with Skipper. She's totally rad and knows the latest must-have apps.

10. Fly a plane. Fight fires. Teach someone to swim. Whip up a delicious vanilla oat milk latte. Fill a cavity. Play in a rock band. Just me? Diversified interests are the name of the game! I like surprising people with my unexpected know-how and versatility! Again, I've asked Barbie for help here and there. Or all the time.

BONUS
Learn how to ask for help.
We all need it!

MOVEMENT IS TOTALLY IN

I've always been a fan of sports
and exercise, whether that's a
touch football game on a Sunday
afternoon or a long run around
the neighborhood. I even won a
few gold medals back in 1976.

Physical activity isn't just about a good-looking physique. It's a great way to deal with stress, get your heart pumping, challenge yourself, and have fun. And the mental benefits are unbeatable—walk the dog, ride bikes with Barbie, play beach volleyball, lift weights a few times a week, or take a yoga class. Or better yet—all of the above! Establish a routine that works for you and stick to it.

What do *I* do in the gym? Anything and everything, depending on the day—and playlist. I love watching and playing soccer, and I've also been known to play tennis doubles with Barbie.

Couple exercise with other self-care rituals, whatever fits your lifestyle! Sure, a spa day is nice, but real well-being lies within taking care of your emotions and surrounding yourself with your crew—though I never turn down a trip to the spa with Barbie. When you treat your body well, you sleep better, you feel better, and you can *be* better for the people in your life.

Lifeguard Ken knows what I'm talking about. Did someone say Beach?

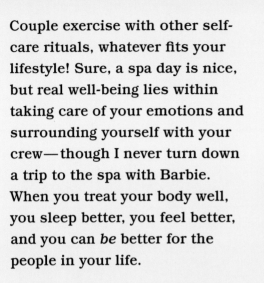

Let's get moving!

25

ANOTHER MAJOR KEN TIP: GET OUTSIDE!

Getting outside in nature is the ultimate mood lift. The sun and plants make us happier. Whatever you choose to do outside, whether it be the cold mountains (I love a good ski moment — an après ski with Barbie is the best), the desert plains (Western Ken enjoys his sun too), or your backyard with Tanner (splashing in the puppy pool), it's important to get outside. But the beach . . . the beach is where I thrive.

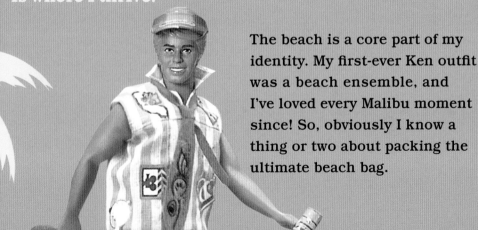

The beach is a core part of my identity. My first-ever Ken outfit was a beach ensemble, and I've loved every Malibu moment since! So, obviously I know a thing or two about packing the ultimate beach bag.

Let me enlighten you.

FIRST AND FOREMOST: SUNSCREEN. Nothing less than SPF 30. Reapply it every two hours, and no, I don't care what the '70s Kens say about sunscreen! Being a Ken is all about responsible sun protection.

A BEACH BLANKET, preferably one that coordinates with my trunks and sandals. It's all in the details.

A FEW PAIRS OF SUNGLASSES, because what if you lose one in the ocean while catching a big wave?

LOTS OF WATER. There's nothing worse than sweating it out playing beach volleyball with nothing to quench your thirst after.

FLIP-FLOPS to keep your real shoes from getting all sandy. The *worst!* Just make sure to find a pair that supports your flat feet.

A GREAT BOOK. Paperback, digital, audio, it's all good. No, there hasn't been an Author Ken . . . yet.

BANDAGES. A good Ken is prepared for anything.

A PLASTIC BRUSH to zhuzh up your beach waves. (For Kens with real hair, anyway.) If you forget, ask Barbie. She's probably got one. Like me, she likes to be prepared.

HAIR TIES. In case Barbie needs one, or in case you need to pull back your man bun.

A GOOD 'TUDE! Most important thing to pack: your best self for your best buddies.

MY LIKES...

SUNSHINE

ROLLERBLADING ON THE BEACH

PLAYING WITH THE DOGS

CONVERTIBLES

VESTS

DISCO

LEARNING NEW SKILLS

STATEMENT ACCESSORIES

...and Barbie!

Build your own list!

AND DISLIKES

SEAWEED

RAINY DAYS

CLEANING THE
HORSE BARN

SCOOTERS

SHOES WITH TIES

SAD MOVIES

SITTING AT HOME

BLENDING IN

All Ken, all ten out of ten.

HAPPY

EMBARRASSED

SAD

CONFUSED

HOPEFUL

TIRED

GRUMPY

EXCITED

Friends Forever

Without friendship, where would we be? Friends are the cornerstone of a healthy life.

I love my crew, especially Barbie and Allan, and nothing makes me happier than spending quality time with my nearest and dearest—including Tanner and Taffy, the adorable Labrador dogs. (Although picking up after Tanner does get old after a while.)

You can find friends anywhere and everywhere, trust me. If you're on the lookout for a new pal or three, there are plenty of places to start looking.

The beach. Duh.

AT WORK OR SCHOOL. You spend eight hours a day, five days a week with these people. It's impossible not to get close with them! Welcome a new teammate or classmate with a happy hour or lunch.

A LOCAL MEETUP GROUP. Bond over shared interests, like karaoke, bowling, a dog breed, or a favorite video game.

MUTUAL FRIENDS. Some of my best pals are those I met via Barbie, like Teresa, Daisy, and Brooklyn. Don't be shy about attending a party where you barely know anyone. Your new best friend could be hanging by the hors d'oeuvres.

ONLINE. It's not just for dating! You can expand your social circle via all the platforms; find online communities that you click with.

THE DOG PARK. If your pups click, you might too.

MEET ALLAN

Have you met my best pal, Allan? (He also goes by Alan, depending on which version you're referring to.) He's the coolest. Allan joined the Barbie crew in 1964, just a few years after me, and we're so close we can even share clothes.

Barbie and her besties are always spotted doing fun stuff together, like hanging by the pool or going dancing, but Allan and I weren't exactly off starring in the *Nutcracker* together. We had to *make* time for each other! Dudes, make it a priority to spend quality time with the other dudes in your life.

To be a well-rounded Ken, you need to have a solid crew of friends who lift you up and encourage you but aren't afraid to call you out when you're acting silly. Who would *you* call in the middle of the night when you're sick, hurt, or stressed out?

Let that person know you appreciate them, and better yet, be there when they need a hand.

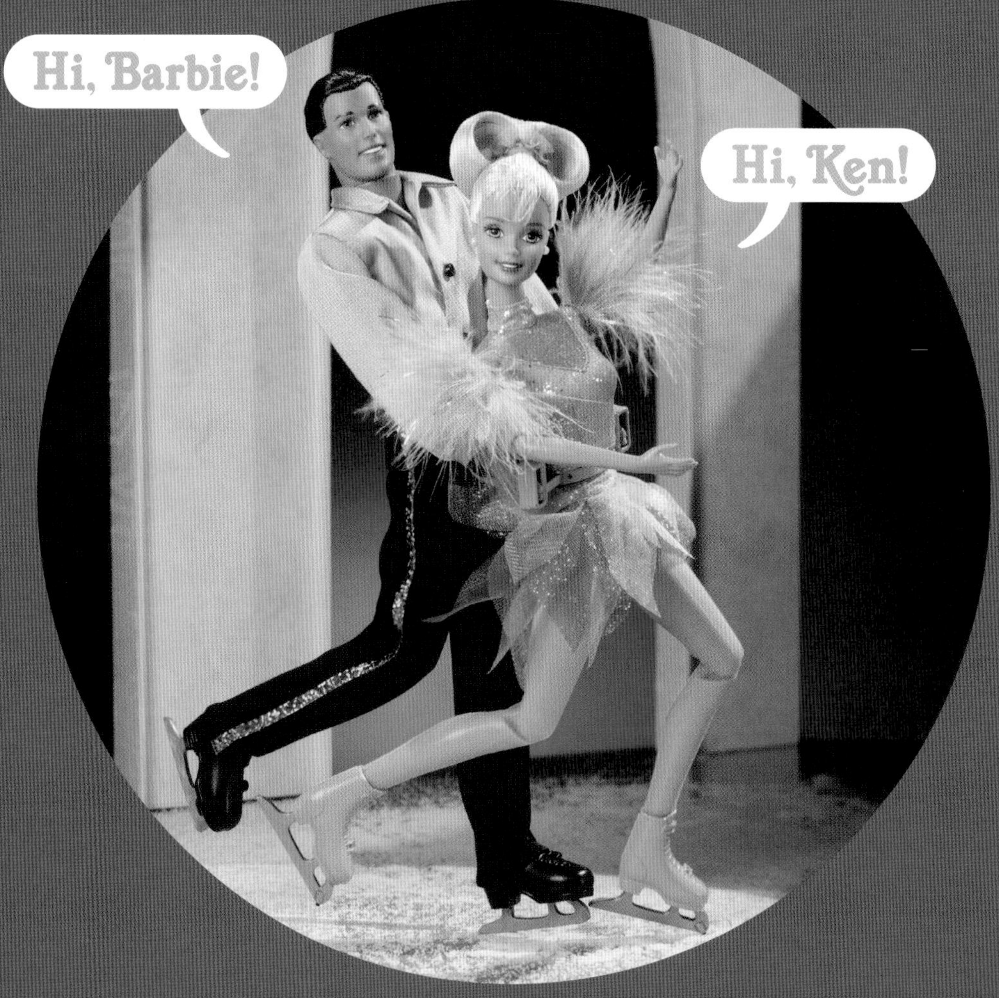

Hi, Barbie!
Hi, Ken!

WHEN KEN MET BARBIE

Let's travel back in time to the day I met Barbie. It was 1961. I rolled up to a party in our Wisconsin hometown looking dapper as can be in my tuxedo and there she was, in a shiny party dress and fur stole. (This was way before the Malibu DreamHouse; we're actually Midwesterners, dontcha know?) Instant friend.

I knew right then and there we were going to be in each other's lives forever. Oh, and did I mention this was also a TV commercial? There was a lot at stake, but we nailed it.

And Barbie? Well, it's Barbie! What can I say that hasn't already been said? I wasn't just impressed by her outfit and her hairstyle, either. She is a great actor, and an even better friend.

FINDING THE BARBIE TO YOUR KEN

Barbie and I have gone through some ups and downs over the years. No matter what our relationship status is, though, I know I have a good friend in her, and she can say the same for me. We love and support each other through new jobs, new hairstyles, fun fashion, and everything in between.

Though some say that Barbie and I can't just be friends, I don't agree! Barbie and I are a stellar example of a strong friendship.

Friendship is a two-way street, and Barbie is as supportive to me as I am to her. She's always inviting me on epic road trips and to glamorous dance parties. I know her well enough to recognize when it's a good time to drop by to say hi and when to give her some space.

Friendship is a two-way street.

It's not complicated.

Great friends push each other to be the best they can be. They also cheer the loudest at every milestone. I know Barbie is always in my corner. And she knows I'm always going to be there for her, no matter what. I just like being around her, and if she needs my help while she's busy running the world, well, here's a hand!

If feelings get complicated—and it *does* happen!—the best thing to do is be honest. Don't force anything; if your feelings aren't reciprocated, that can hurt, but don't take it out on the other person. Take some time apart, get some clarity, and move on as best you can.

Ken in L·O·V·E
DATING AND RELATIONSHIPS

Dating has changed a lot since Barbie and I first came onto the scene, and as all close relationships do, ours has evolved over the decades. Whether we're dating or not, I'm just happy to be here — and that's all part of the fun. We've had more than 60 years of experience, so you probably wanna listen in.

DATING PROFILE 101

These days, you're more likely to meet someone on your phone than you are on the set of a TV commercial. (Weird. Can't relate!)

Feeling good!

Getting someone to swipe right on you is harder than it seems since so much of dating has moved online in the past few years, so it's also important to learn how to be courteous digitally. It's a balancing act of curating compelling info without overdoing it and presenting yourself in your best light without coming off as fake or conceited.

It's overwhelming, I know. But you're a Ken, and you Ken do this.

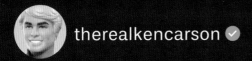
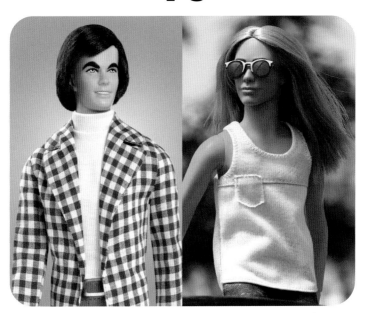

Pics my mom posts of me **VS** What they see on my social

A FEW RULES OF THUMB

CHOOSE A FEW GOOD PICS of you solo. Don't make potential love interests guess which groomsman you are. Think casual snaps, not your work headshot. Don't be afraid to ask your friends to snap a few pics! That's what friends are for.

BE KIND AND POSITIVE on your profile and when you're chatting. Snide, sarcastic language is a red flag.

IS IT A MATCH? Start the convo with an engaging question based off *their* profile or a genuine, "Hi! How's it going?" and go from there.

IF SOMEONE TURNS YOU DOWN, try not to take it too personally. You barely know each other! Just swipe on.

Let's take a look at that profile ...

BE CONFIDENT but not cocky. If you overdo it trying to impress somebody, you'll probably do the opposite.

WHEN YOU'RE PICKING UP an "I'm interested" vibe, don't waste time messaging endlessly. Make a plan and get together IRL.

AND REMEMBER, you can always ask Barbie for help putting it together. She's always given me good pointers. (Examples: "Maybe get rid of the fish picture?" and "Add the picture of you at the beach!" Things like that.)

SPARK A CONVERSATION

SIMPLE WAYS TO GET TO KNOW SOMEONE

Whether you're swiping online, betting on a blind date, or hanging with a crush, the best thing to do at first is to be genuinely interested in the person you're talking to. Even if there isn't a spark — and there may not be! — you may end up making a great new friend or professional connection.

BE A GOOD LISTENER. Share your own personal experiences when they're relevant; just don't spend the conversation talking about yourself.

ASK GOOD QUESTIONS. If they bring up something that sounds interesting, ask them to elaborate. Talk about the movies you've seen, books you've read, an old TV show you just discovered and binged in a day, or that weeklong trip to Europe. Do you have mutual friends or connections? That's a great way to get the conversation flowing.

PLAN AN ACTIVITY you both enjoy. Figure out your common ground and start there. Perhaps you both like rock climbing or reading. Maybe you're both great cooks, or big into home renovation.

BE PRESENT. Don't multitask or stare at your phone when you're together. Put the distractions away and give them your undivided attention.

If you're not vibing, don't force it; be honest about it. Be kind and respectful when you know it's not working for you. Wish them well and don't drag things out. If they're not feeling you, accept it graciously and move on.

If you *are* vibing, let them know you're interested! Don't play games. Clear communication is always appreciated. Plan another meetup. Tell them you're having fun and want to keep seeing each other.

I'll meet you on the dance floor in five minutes.

You should also know by now that there's no such thing as a good pickup line. What *does* capture someone's interest? Two things: a compliment you really mean, like "You are such a great role model, Barbie!" and a promise they know you'll keep, like "I'll meet you on the dance floor in five minutes" or "Let's get together on Friday at 7 PM. I'll get tickets to the show."

Yes, it really can be that simple. Genuine and trustworthy signals that you're a total keeper.

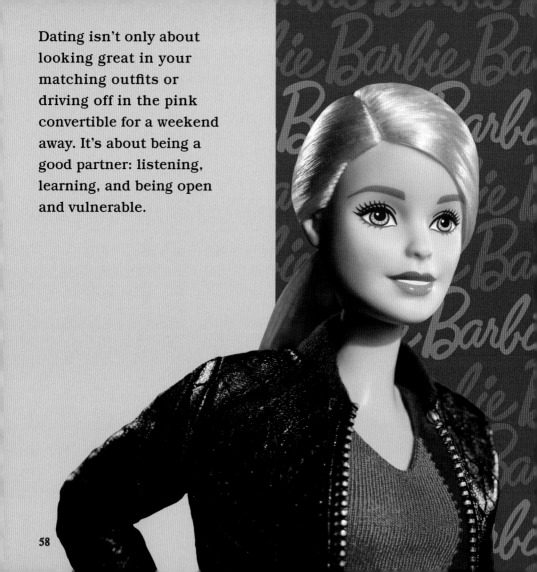

Dating isn't only about looking great in your matching outfits or driving off in the pink convertible for a weekend away. It's about being a good partner: listening, learning, and being open and vulnerable.

When you're upset, the best way to work through it is to talk it out. And when you're happy, celebrate together. Build them up and cheer them on, and they'll do the same for you.

THOUGHTFUL GESTURES

IT'S ALL ABOUT THE LITTLE THINGS

SURPRISE THEM with their favorite coffee and breakfast food in the morning.

PICK UP FLOWERS just because. Learn their favorite colors and blooms in advance so you can grab the perfect bouquet.

IF THEY MENTION wanting to see a certain movie or check out a new restaurant, take note and plan a date night around it.

DID YOU READ A BOOK they might enjoy or hear a song that reminds you of them? Drop off a copy or send them a link to the song with a "Thinking of you" text.

MAKE AN EFFORT with their friends. Best case scenario, they'll become your friends too.

WHEN THEY'RE STRESSED at work, drop off dinner or send them a gift card for delivery and take one thing off their full plate.

Thanks, Ken!

LEND A HELPING HAND when they need it. Don't push your way into a sticky situation or overstep boundaries, but when someone needs assistance— say, their Wi-Fi is out and you know your way around a router— step in and do your part.

REMEMBER BIRTHDAYS and anniversaries. Plug it into your phone calendar and set a reminder so you never forget. Easy!

THE ART OF COMPROMISE

In life and love, you may not always see eye to eye with your chosen person. Wouldn't it be boring if you agreed on everything 100% of the time?

Let's knock it off and talk it out!

In these instances you have to learn how to compromise, otherwise you risk hurt feelings, resentment, and anger. That doesn't mean giving in entirely! You make progress when you work to meet in the middle.

When you step outside of your comfort zone and put yourself out there, magic happens. Barbie is into trying new things; she's always changing careers, helping others, redecorating the DreamHouse, and traveling to snowy peaks and desert ranches. When I'm with her, I know one thing for sure: it won't be boring!

Don't be afraid to jump on the makeover train when it rolls into town. Barbie has always kept up with all the trends. When she embraced change, I embraced change. When she handed me the satin-trimmed gym shorts and roller skates, I grabbed my boom box and hit the rink. I've learned you can't fight the disco, so you might as well have fun with it!

Embrace the change.

I benefited from these changes too. When Barbie wanted to spend more time on the beaches of Malibu, I practiced my surfing skills and got a job—Beach. (The tan didn't hurt either.)

In any type of relationship, remember that change is inevitable. Trying new things and growing together is part of what keeps life interesting.

BEST GIFTS FOR BARBIE

Whether the Barbie in your life is your true love or your best pal, giving them a gift is *never* a bad idea.

SOME KEN-APPROVED PICKS:

FRESH PLANTS OR FLOWERS. Liven up their DreamHouse with some color and greenery.

A CUTE NEW LEASH for their dog, especially if it matches a favorite pair of sneakers.

COZY SWEATERS, perfect for nighttime serenades on the beach or early morning walks.

A CAR WASH. Don't underestimate acts of love like washing the car. There's something extra special about someone doing that for you, so volunteer to take the convertible in for a thorough cleaning.

ART. Once you've figured out their taste, a small piece of art from a local artist or photographer is always a thoughtful, meaningful gift.

A playlist you made just for them.

THE BUZZY BOOK you keep hearing about. Read it together. Love it or hate it, it'll spark discussion.

SOMETHING FOR THEIR HOME that you know they need; a pro tip is to keep a running list when they mention they want a new pink toaster or teapot. Next time it's time to gift, you're good to go.

YOUR TIME! Time is the best gift you can give.

PLANNING A DREAM DATE

The key word here is *planning*. As in you do the work, not your partner!

Here's what you gotta do to bring a Dream Date to life. Trust me, it's not that hard. It just requires a little foresight.

1 Think of an activity you would both enjoy equally. A cooking class, fancy dinner, snowboarding, renting a kayak, whatever! You know yourself and your partner best. Emphasis on something you'd *both* enjoy; don't take them to a baseball game when you know they love soccer...

2 Make the necessary reservations in a timely fashion so you're not scrambling last minute.

3 Tell your partner any relevant details: date, time, location, and where you'll meet or what time you'll pick them up.

4 Enjoy your time together.

Moo-hoo.

But what if the Dream Date goes wrong? Even the best laid plans aren't foolproof. Maybe your dinner wasn't great — go out for ice cream after and save the day. If the activity you thought would be an instant hit kinda fizzled, well, better luck next time. Your partner will appreciate the fact that you put in the work to plan something special for them, and that's what counts.

LIFE DOESN'T ALWAYS GO AS PLANNED

DEALING WITH THE TOUGH STUFF

Life in BarbieLand isn't all pastel scenery and dance parties. We go through rough patches just like everyone else. But Kens like us look on the bright side. When a tragedy befalls you, see how you can turn a negative into a positive and learn from it.

HOW TO DEAL WITH REJECTION AND BREAKUPS

It happens to the best of us. When it happened to me, all I wanted was to run away and hide from the spotlight. I felt lost and alone ... until I realized I learned a lot through rejection. I had to learn to be my own person, and that made me stronger and more confident.

Take time away from it all. Mourn. Grieve. Work on yourself, get introspective. Call Allan.

What about a fresh haircut? Sometimes a physical change can get you out of a rut.

Give yourself time and space to feel your feelings, then pick yourself up, stretch out, and try again. This is the time for self-discovery. Who are you without Barbie? What do you want? Who do you want to be? Figuring these things out will make your next relationship better—and it'll make *you* better too.

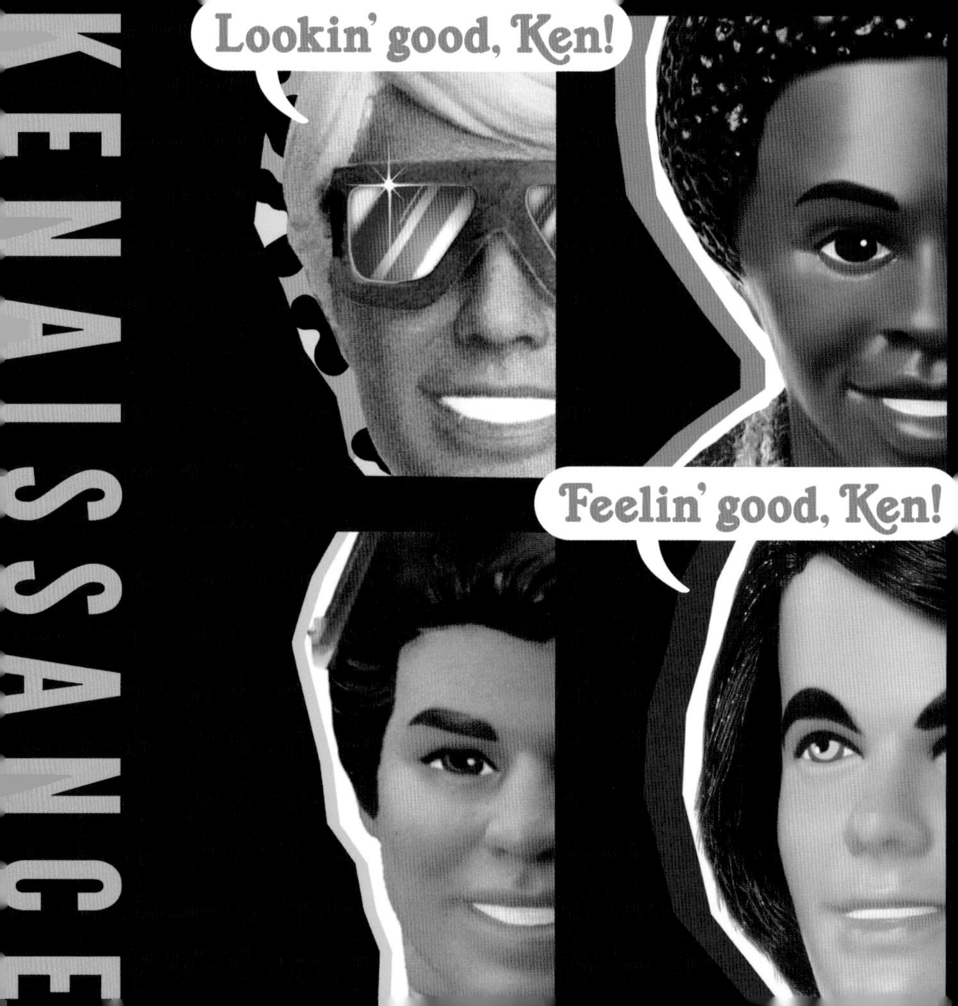
KENAISSANCE
Lookin' good, Ken!
Feelin' good, Ken!

KEN COUTURE

Ken Style

Back in the day, I was all about the formal suits and fantastic swimwear, but these days, I like to express myself through all different types of clothes! Just like Barbie, I like having different options when it comes to outfits. Trying new clothes is one of my passions. It may not be everyone's cup of tea, but if you want to be a little more like Ken, you might want to think about your personal style. I love a studded (or sequined) power suit, but I feel equally great in a neon hoodie, a sharp polo, or a denim jacket.

Sure, I've fallen victim to a few trends over the years, but hey, I had fun, and that's what it's all about, right? Maybe those acid wash joggers will come back in style again someday soon, and I'll be ready and waiting. They're still in my closet, obviously.

Style is all about figuring out what *you* feel good in, not what everyone else is wearing. There's a reason they call it personal style.

Trends are fun, but they're not forever. Figure out the foundation of your look and then experiment when it feels authentic to you. If you're an outdoorsy Ken, show your love of adventure with a plaid shirt, lightweight pants, and trusty boots. Maybe try adding a pop of color— I love my hot-pink puffer jacket. If you're more of an indoor Ken, find a pulled-together way to show your laid-back style like worn-in denim with a cozy Henley. Whatever makes you feel good!

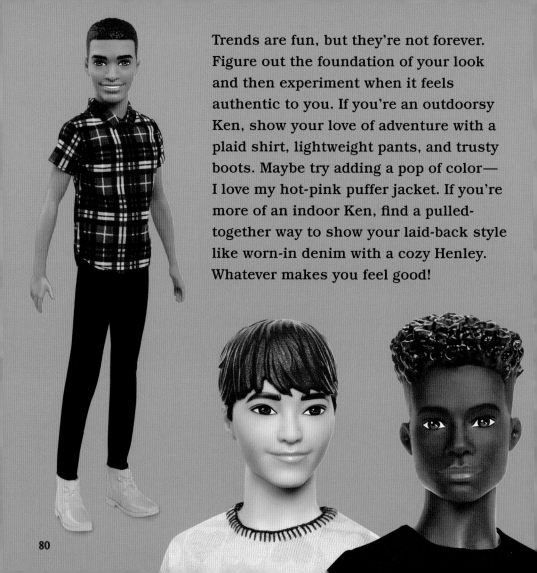

More into glamming up than dressing down? Even better! Kens *love* a tuxedo. In fact, I'd call it one of my signature looks. No matter what you're wearing, the key is confidence, and confidence comes with knowing what makes you, you.

Let's take a peek at some of my signature looks, shall we? That'll help you get started on this journey we call fashion.

MEET THE KEN CLASSICS

No closet is complete without these must-have pieces. I like to call these my tried-and-true essentials. You know, the "buy once and wear forever" kinda thing.

A TUXEDO. Cummerbund optional, but I find it adds a certain je ne sais quoi to a formal ensemble. If you're out and about with Barbie, give her a call and see what she's wearing before you plan your outfit, then match her color scheme with your tie or a boutonniere. I prefer a classic black tux, but I've been known to wear all shades of the rainbow. Sometimes all shades of the rainbow at once.

A SPORT COAT. Any color will do: black, navy, plaid, Power Pink, and turquoise. You know, just in case. This works with jeans, trousers, shorts, a mermaid tail, or whatever sparks your fancy when dialing up your look.

SHORTS AND A TANK TOP. For the beach, obviously. Or hanging out poolside at the DreamHouse. Some of my most iconic outfits are my beach looks, so it's near and dear to my heart and the kind of 'fit that never goes out of style. I prefer short shorts that hit several inches above the knee for a classic appeal.

WESTERN WEAR. You never know when Barbie will invite you line dancing or want to go horseback riding. Plus, you can never go wrong with fringe!

VESTS. A vest can take you anywhere. I like denim, dressy, and casual. They all have a prime spot in my rotation.

With the right wardrobe, it's easy to transform your look from AM to PM. A true Ken closet is versatile and ready for anything: a trip to space, a backyard barbecue, a soccer game, or a giant blowout party.

HAIR AND SELF-CARE

There's no such thing as one-hairstyle-fits-all in the Ken world. Back in the day, my hair was fully plastic and shellacked to my head, but we've updated it with the times. I got my first real hair in the '70s, and since then, I've rocked all kinds of styles, from totally cool waves in the '90s to a man bun in the '10s.

Personally, I think every look I've worn was totally cool, even the ones that feel a *bit* dated today. I've also experimented with facial hair; who could forget my 1973 Mod Hair with thick, luscious locks and stick-on sideburns?

Hair there and everywhere!

WHEN THE HAIR IS

ON POINT

Make sure your SPF game is strong.

I've said it once, and I'll say it again, whether you're soaking on the beach or playing a game of pickleball, make sure you're wearing sunscreen. It's not just for Barbie; it's for everyone!

Oh, and watch the cologne. Too much of a good thing can sometimes not play in your favor. One to two sprays is enough. Trust me.

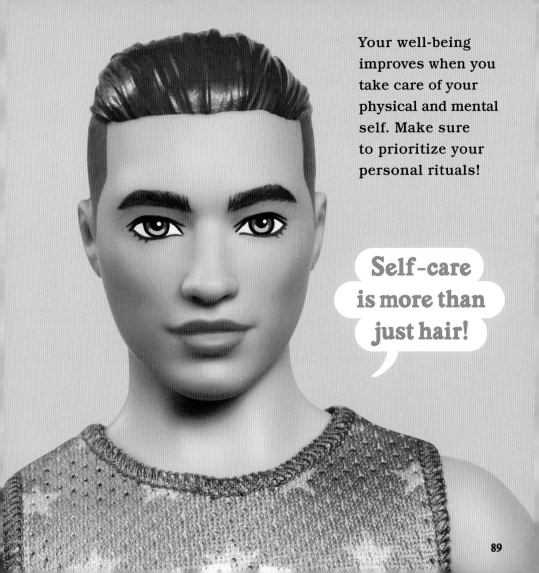

Your well-being improves when you take care of your physical and mental self. Make sure to prioritize your personal rituals!

Self-care is more than just hair!

ACCESSORIES MAKE THE OUTFIT

Never underestimate the power of a well-placed accessory! When your 'fit is looking a bit blah, add a hat, a scarf, or maybe even a giant silver earring and necklace. (Wink-wink.)

The Ken closet is *nothing* without accessories. I've got cowboy hats for horseback riding and square dancing, colorful skates for a day on the boardwalk, a statement tie to impress, scarves for a flourish, snappy dress shoes for dancing and dining, even tiny sunglasses.

Accessories make a good outfit great, and a great outfit can take you anywhere. Even to the moon!

LEFT TO RIGHT:

Ken Ken Ken Ken

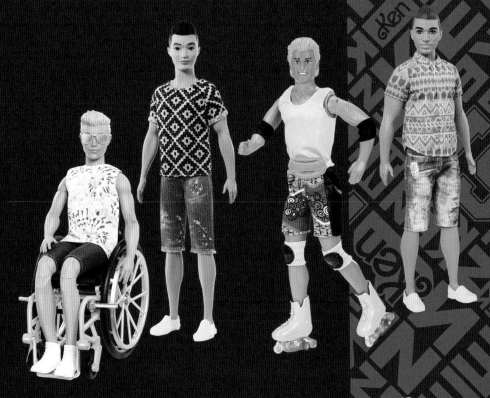

Ken Ken Ken Ken

Final Thoughts

FROM KEN

Thanks for coming on this journey of self-discovery with me. Some of you have been around since the '60s, and some are probably just discovering the wonder and joy of Ken. Kens like us are pretty cool, right? It's time to get up, stand proud, and remember who you are.

I'm the ultimate Barbie fan, but you can be a number one fan AND be true to yourself.

Consider this your final pep talk as you embark on your quest to become your best Ken. You've got this! Armed with the wisdom I've so thoughtfully shared here—wisdom I picked up over the last 60+ years—there's nothing you can't do.

When you're feeling less than confident, do what I do: turn on your favorite playlist, get dressed in your favorite clothes, and soak up some sunshine with your friends.

I bet you my beach towel that your mood will turn around immediately.

It's easy to get caught up in the "more, more, more" mindset of our current times, but a Ken like me knows that cool sunglasses, the perfect all-over tan, a flashy car, or a fur coat doesn't make the person.

Being kind, thoughtful, and genuine is what it's all about. And that's where real confidence begins.

Always remember this:

You may simply be Ken. But you're also an icon.

ACKNOWLEDGMENTS

First off, I'd like to thank Barbie. My best pal, better half, fashion icon, soulmate, and life inspiration. Thank you to my dearest buddy, Allan. Yes, you can borrow that sweater.

Big thanks to Tanner the dog for all those walks. They really helped me focus on completing this book.

And most of all, thanks to anyone creating their own Ken stories, bringing my dreams—and yours—to life.

Stay beachy, *Ken*™

KARA NESVIG covers pop culture, celebrity, beauty, and style for publications including *Teen Vogue*, *Allure*, *People*, and *Brides*, and is the author of many pop culture decks. She lives in Minnesota with her husband, son, and Cavalier King Charles Spaniel.